"Elizabeth Achtemeier does not pretend that the task of searching for an able and faithful preacher is easy, but she does h^{el} to make the task clearer, mor[~] ┄ l more deeply rooted '   "

                                             G
                              ╌gical Seminary

". . . So interesting that I read it all in one sitting. I can't count the number of pulpit committees that I wish had read this book and paid attention to its advice. Somewhere a church is going to have a better experience of ministry because it followed the counsel of *So You're Looking for a New Preacher.*"

— CLYDE E. FANT
Stetson University

So You're Looking for a New Preacher

A Guide for
Pulpit Nominating Committees

Elizabeth Achtemeier

William B. Eerdmans Publishing Company
Grand Rapids, Michigan

Copyright © 1991 by Wm. B. Eerdmans Publishing Co.

255 Jefferson Ave. S.E., Grand Rapids, Mich. 49503

Printed in the United States of America

Library of Congress Cataloging-in-Publication Data

Achtemeier, Elizabeth Rice, 1926–
So you're looking for a new preacher: a guide for pulpit
nominating committees / Elizabeth Achtemeier.
p.   cm.
ISBN 0-8028-0596-5
1. Pastoral search committees.   I. Title.
II. Title: So you are looking for a new preacher.
BV664.A26   1991
254 — dc20   91-24603
CIP

Contents

v

Preface

This little book is intended to help pulpit nominating committees select good *preachers* to call to their pulpits. Most church members rank preaching as their highest priority in selecting a minister to lead them. Yet far too often PNCs are uncertain about how to separate good preaching from bad.

Because I teach preaching in a theological seminary, and because I critique dozens — sometimes many dozens — of sermons every year, it occurred to me that I might pass on in writing some criteria which PNCs can use to assess preachers and their sermon content and delivery.

The first section of this book, "How to Organize a Pulpit Nominating Committee," is rather brief. It gives PNCs just a few guidelines about how to get organized and what general procedures to follow. Because I want this book to be useful for all denominations, I do not elaborate the specific procedures of any particular denomination.

The second section of the book, "How to Find a Good Preacher," is the more important of the two for my purposes. My primary interest is in helping you to find a preacher for your pulpit who will effectively and faithfully preach the Gospel of Jesus Christ. If this book helps just one PNC to do that, it will have served its purpose.

I pray that God will guide your search.

Union Theological Seminary   Elizabeth Achtemeier
Richmond, Virginia

Introduction

Congratulations on being selected to serve on your congregation's pulpit nominating committee! The members of your church are entrusting you with a great responsibility, and they must have a great deal of confidence in your good judgment, for there are few tasks more important to the church's life than that of calling a new minister to a pulpit.

The person you call will do many things in your congregation. He or she will not only preach but will also be your pastor, ministering to you during times of sorrow and beside your bed of pain. Your pastor will baptize believers into Christ and feed them with the body and blood of our Lord. He or she will preside over weddings, and will comfort with the news of resurrection at the side of a freshly dug grave.

Your pastor will be your shepherd during the most intimate moments of your life, guiding you, comforting you, sometimes admonishing you in the name of the Lord.

Equally important, the minister you call will be responsible for educating your congregation, teaching and training others to teach your adults and children, your women and men what it means to be a Christian in our time.

In addition, your minister will represent your church in your community and enlist you in service to others. She or he will guide your church's mission to the world as part of the universal church. By your minister's gifts of planning and vision and leadership, your offerings of time and talent and money will often be apportioned. By his or her wisdom and care, your congregation's programs and activities will largely be guided.

Your minister will live in your midst as preacher, educator, administrator, youth leader, catechetical instructor, worship leader, social activist, churchgoer, fellow Christian, and friend. The list of a modern minister's roles could be expanded almost endlessly.

But nothing that your minister does will be more important than preaching. Consider for a moment: The first impression that visitors to and potential members of your congregation will have of your church will be formed largely by what they hear from your pulpit. The whole tone and direction of your congregation's life will be determined by what your minister preaches. Either the content of his or her sermons will feed you weekly with the Bread of Life, or the lack of content will starve you spiritually and mentally. Indeed, either your future preacher will inspire your congregation to have faith in Christ and to grow up into the measure of the fullness of Christ's grace — or your future preacher will leave you dead in spirit and devoid of growth in the Christian life.

"Faith comes from what is heard," writes Paul, "and what is heard comes by the preaching of Christ" (Rom. 10:17). But "how are they to hear without a preacher" (v. 14)? As a member of the pulpit nominating committee, you have an enormously important task!

> Direct us, O Lord, in all our doings with thy most gracious favor, and further us with thy continual help; that in all our works begun, continued, and ended in thee, we may glorify thy holy name, and finally by thy mercy obtain everlasting life; through Jesus Christ our Lord. Amen.

I

How to Organize a Pulpit Nominating Committee

Getting Started

Every denomination has its own process by which it aids its churches in finding a new minister, and you will want to be thoroughly acquainted with that process so that you can follow it and cooperate with it. It can be of enormous help to you.

You probably have been chosen to serve on the pulpit nominating committee because together you represent a cross-section of your congregation. If you do not know each other, you will have to spend some time getting acquainted, and you should try to get to know one another well. There will be nothing more vital to your proper functioning than your trust of one another. You are going to have to agree on one candidate for your pulpit, and you all will have to stand behind the recommendation of that candidate to your congregation. PNCs are no place for secret agendas, hidden reservations, personal backbiting, or power struggles. If Christian love, patience, kindness, candor, and graciousness are to be found anywhere, they should be found in PNCs. To foster the creation of that Christian unity, pray together to God for that gift.

But also pray to God to lead you in your search. Christian ministers are not *hired* by congregations; they are *called* to serve congregations — called by God and his church. If you pray to God for guidance, he will work through you to find the person he desires to have in your pulpit. Never meet together without that sincere prayer, and carry that prayer in your hearts when you are apart.

Before you begin searching for a minister, make sure you know your congregation's needs and character. Some churches conduct self-studies before they begin looking for a new preacher, and such self-studies are helpful — not only to the PNC but also to the candidate whom you choose. There is a "fit" that must obtain between a minister and a congregation if the minister is truly to lead the congregation. A preacher who is primarily charismatic will be like a fish out of water in some congregations;

one who emphasizes only social action will not fit in others. The ideal, of course, is to find a minister who preaches the whole Gospel and who brings a balance to your congregation's life. Nevertheless, some candidates will be more suited to your church than others, and the only way you can know that is to analyze and know in detail where your congregation is on its spiritual journey and what type of congregation it is.

If there are more than three of you, you will need a chairperson to moderate your discussion, preferably one who knows parliamentary procedure. You will need one person to take careful notes on your deliberations. And you especially will need someone to take charge of the dossiers, recommendations, correspondence, and sermon tapes that you receive. You will also need access to a copying machine so that copies of dossiers and correspondence can be circulated among all of your committee members.

It is very important to *acknowledge by letter all dossiers and tapes that you receive* so that candidates know their material has been received. It is also exceedingly important, and a matter of common courtesy, to *let a candidate know when he or she is no longer under consideration*. Some candidates send dossiers to PNCs and then never hear another word from them, leaving the hopeful candidate uncertain about any plans for the future.

Your church governing board or session should tell you how much money you have available for visits to churches, for long-distance phone calls, for postage, and for other administrative costs. They also should give you a written statement of the terms of call that gives an initial job description of the position you are filling and includes the annual salary, housing arrangements, travel allowance, insurance, medical benefits, and vacation and study times. You may also want to supplement the description of your congregation that you give to candidates with information about your community and geographical area. Often you can obtain pamphlets and descriptive folders from the chamber of commerce or other civic organizations; there is no reason for you to duplicate the work they have already done.

It cannot be emphasized too strongly that all of your deliberations and all of the information that you gather about candidates for your pulpit *must remain confidential and confined within your committee.* You can ruin someone's life or undermine her or his ministry by spreading information outside of your committee. If church members ask how your work is progressing, tell them only that it is in process but mention no names or other particulars. After you have completed your work, destroy all information you have received about other candidates who have not been called. You must be absolutely trustworthy on this score.

Determining the Process You Will Use

You need an organized procedure by which you will assess candidates for your pulpit. The following list of steps may be helpful:

1. Develop lists of possible candidates for the position and gather dossiers, sermon tapes, and recommendations.
2. Carefully read dossiers and initial recommendations, beginning to eliminate some candidates.
3. Arrange telephone interviews with possible candidates to determine their interest and availability, to introduce yourselves and your church and your needs, and to begin sounding out the candidates on their views. It is helpful to conduct these interviews by speaker phone so that two of you can talk to a candidate at the same time. Set up the interview ahead of time. Know the questions you want to ask and the information you want to convey. Take careful notes on what

11

is said. What you learn in these interviews will help you continue your elimination process. (This weeding-out process continues throughout the next steps.)

4. Gather in-depth recommendations and references for the remaining candidates so that you have at your disposal as much information about them as possible.

5. Listen to sermon tapes. If a certain candidate has not sent a tape, request one.

6. Set up personal interviews with the (small) list of candidates remaining. Set forth the terms of call at this time.

7. Arrange to visit churches to hear the candidates in their pulpits. If a candidate is a recent seminary graduate and serves no church regularly, request that he or she be allowed to preach in a neutral pulpit in your area.

8. Interview the candidates with their families.

9. Select one candidate to call to your pulpit.

10. Arrange for the chosen candidate to meet with your church board or session.

11. If the board or session agrees with your choice, unanimously recommend one candidate to your congregation.

12. Have the candidate preach a sermon from your pulpit. (Some denominations do not take this

step, relying solely on the recommendation of the PNC and the approval by the governing board of the church. I think it is much wiser to let the whole congregation hear the candidate, because they are finally the ones who are calling him or her.)

13. Have the congregation vote on calling the candidate. The moderator of the congregational meeting should try to secure a unanimous vote. If there are many objections, the candidate should not be called and, indeed, should not want to accept the call.

When you have called your candidate and he or she has accepted, celebrate and thank God!

The procedure you follow is important — but how do you assess your candidates? Let us now look at some criteria that may help you find a really fine preacher for your congregation.

II

How to Find a Good Preacher

Pitfalls and Perils for PNCs

You probably already have some thoughts in the back of your mind about the kind of person you would like to see in your pulpit. But before you become totally committed to your ideas, you should be aware of some of the pitfalls and perils in choosing a preacher.

Preaching well is a great labor. That is the chief reason it does not happen very often. . . . People are dying of triviality.

— Gerard Sloyan, *Worshipful Preaching*

✠ *Do not try to find someone who is just like your beloved former pastor or, for that matter, who is the opposite of the preacher you had before.* One congregation, I am told, had a rather gruff and introspective minister for several years, and so the next time around they looked for a jolly, outgoing type. They ended up with a jokester in their pulpit who could tell entertaining little moral stories but whose sermons had no depth. The members slowly starved for the Word and began drifting away to other churches. Another congregation suffered for a period of years under a minister who was rather intellectually dull; their next choice was a Ph.D. He wore his academic robe in the pulpit every Sunday, but he simply could not preach.

Forget the former minister when you are looking for a new one. "Remember not the former things," God says in Isaiah. "Behold, I am doing a new thing" (43:18-19). Start fresh and search for the best preacher you can find.

Do not set arbitrary limits on age and experience. Some established congregations determine ahead of time that they will consider only those candidates who have ten or more years of experience in the pastorate. While experience is valuable, especially in those larger churches that have multiple administrative tasks, it is not a sure guide to a minister's com-

16

petence. A preacher who has been in the field for a number of years may have ceased to learn and may be preaching the same basic message over and over. Conversely, a person who has been out of seminary for just four or five years may be much more energetic and may have many more leadership skills and many more insights into the mysteries of the Gospel than a "veteran" in the church. Similarly, do not overlook those beyond a certain age. A fifty-nine-year-old may be able to bring to your pulpit insights from a long life of faithfulness that will enrich your congregation for years, even after he or she is no longer with you.

There is something in the very tone of the man who has been with Jesus which has more power to touch the heart than the most perfect oratory.

— C. H. Spurgeon, *Lectures to My Students*

In short, avoid setting too many preconditions as you begin your work. Instead, closely examine the individual qualifications of your candidates.

Look beyond gender, race, and physical abilities. Most

17

churches are still hesitant or unwilling to call a woman as their senior pastor. Some are unaware that women served as leaders and preachers for the early church, according to the New Testament (Acts 9:36-43; Rom. 16:1-16; 1 Cor. 11:5; 16:19; 2 Tim. 4:19). Others simply are not used to the idea of a woman in the pulpit, just as many years ago none of us was used to the idea of women announcers on TV. But invariably some of our best preachers and pastors in seminary classes are women, and churches who call women often rave about their leadership. Other congregations would profit greatly from tapping this essentially untouched pool of expertise. There are hundreds of women throughout this country who are graduating from theological seminaries, or who are serving as associate pastors in larger churches, or who are shepherding small rural parishes. Any one of a number of them could be an excellent minister to you.

By the same token, do not automatically rule out someone who is handicapped or of another race than the majority of your parishioners. The Word of God is not bound by color or nationality or physical condition. The best graduate in a seminary class may have had a cleft palate or may be in a wheelchair. The most inspiring preacher may be African-American or Hispanic or Asian or Native American. Look

> *There is neither Jew nor Greek, there is*
> *neither slave nor free, there is neither*
> *male nor female; for you are all one in*
> *Christ Jesus.*
>
> — St. Paul, Galatians 3:28

for the person behind the outward appearance and gender.

Do not be overawed by academic degrees. Certainly your candidate should be a graduate of an accredited seminary, with training in Bible and theology, church history, and pastoral care; ignorance is no advantage in the ministry. But seminaries differ, and seminary records vary widely, and you need to know what lies behind the Master of Divinity (the initial seminary degree), or the Doctor of Ministry, or the Ph.D. Do not hesitate to ask each candidate for his or her seminary transcript, and scrutinize it carefully. Did the candidate barely squeak through seminary training, or did he or she earn all A's or honors? Was the seminary training narrowly focused, or was it preparation for the wide range of ministry?

Each candidate will furnish you with several written recommendations, but remember, those come from the candidate's friends. You may want to write or call some individuals other than those giving initial recommendations — some professors or clergy or laypersons who have worked with the candidate.

Academic degrees are important, but they can also be misleading. A candidate with an M.Div. degree may be more competent than one with a Ph.D. In rare instances, it is possible that a person calling himself or herself "Doctor" has attended only a month-long Doctor of Ministry seminar to earn the title. Or a doctorate may be only honorary. Do some investigation. Ask what an academic degree involved so that later you will not be unpleasantly surprised.

Finally, *do not decide that a candidate's preaching is unimportant compared with his or her other qualifications.* In assessing the life of your congregation, you may decide that what you want above all in your minister is a faithful counselor, or a good teacher, or a strong evangelist, or someone who will attract the young people. All of these qualifications are important, but whatever the qualification you think is primary, remember that the person you call will also have to preach. If you have only one minister, that person will have to preach Sunday after Sunday and special occasion after special occasion. And if the one you choose cannot preach well, every other area of the church's life will suffer because of that failing. Indeed, even if you have two ministers or even several ministers for your congregation, no one is attracted to a counselor or teacher or youth leader or evangelist who is a dud in the pulpit. Preaching carries the church. As Herman Melville wrote in *Moby Dick,* "The world's a ship on its passage out . . . and the pulpit is its prow."

Eloquence is the art of putting into words that which is extremely difficult to put into words. It is the minister of the Word's vocation to be eloquent in this sense.

— R. E. C. Brown,
The Ministry of the Word

Where the pulpit leads, there the church follows, and no matter what his or her other qualifications, if the candidate you choose cannot preach, you will be left adrift on a glassy sea, with no wind of the Spirit to carry you forward toward God's good kingdom of life.

What Is Good Preaching?

Many pulpit nominating committees fail their congregations because they simply do not know what good preaching is. Some members of these committees have never heard a really fine preacher. Others of them carry set ideas about preaching formed in childhood or by previous experience, ideas that may not be helpful because they are too rigid or wrongheaded or both. In order to call a good preacher, you need to know what preaching is supposed to be and do.

Like the sacraments, preaching is a channel through which God works in the midst of his people. It is what we call "a means of grace." And God's

---

Every Sunday morning, when it comes, ought to find [the preacher] awed and thrilled by the reflection — "God is to be in action today, through me, for these people; this day may be crucial, this service decisive, for someone now ripe for the vision of Jesus."

— James Stewart, *Heralds of God*

---

grace is always active. We might even say that God's grace is God's action. It is his judging and forgiving and sustaining and saving work in his world and in his church.

This means that preaching as a means of grace, or as God's action, is never intended simply to communicate information or to give you new ideas about God and yourself and the world, although certainly you receive those when you hear a good sermon. Above all, preaching is never intended simply to entertain you or to pass on to you a good story or a joke that you can share with your neighbors. No. Preaching in the Christian church is one of the channels through which God works immediately on a Sunday morning in the lives of his gathered people.

Good preaching may call some aspect of your lifestyle into question or convey to you the actual forgiveness of God in Christ. It may comfort and strengthen you in sorrow or in trouble, or inspire you to undertake a new course of action in your home or community, or create a new unity with your fellow church members. It may empower you with the Spirit to live by Christ's commandments, or give you an unshakeable certainty of your coming eternal life in the kingdom of God. In short, good preaching leads you into a new or renewed *experience* of the work of God in your life and in the life of your congregation. Good preaching opens the way for God's action and God's changes to be wrought in human hearts and lives. "If anyone is in Christ, [that person] is a new creation," writes Paul (2 Cor. 5:17). Through good preaching, God effects that newness.

Preaching works as a channel of God's active grace only when it is formed by and comes out of the Bible. In the Christian faith, we believe that God revealed himself through his words and deeds in the life of his people Israel and revealed himself supremely in the life, death, and resurrection of Jesus Christ our Lord. Through the events recorded for us in the Old and the New Testament, the one true God drew near to humankind and made himself known and worked his salvation in the person of his Son for all time to come.

But God did not stop acting when his book went to press! He still uses the medium of the Bible to draw near to us and to make himself known and to save us. When we hear the content of the Bible proclaimed and illumined from the pulpit, by the work of the Holy Spirit its events still mediate God's presence and character and actions to us, and Jesus Christ's life and death and resurrection become saving events for us also.

So it is only when a minister preaches from the

Bible that his or her words become God's Word — God's speech and action — to us. Only if preaching comes from the Bible is it a means of grace. Otherwise the preacher's words remain just human words, without God's powerful, saving action working through them by his Spirit.

Obviously, this does not mean that a preacher simply repeats verbatim the words of the Bible or just retells the biblical stories. Often the Bible's content has to be explained. Always it has to be related

---

Apart from serious engagement with the Bible there is simply no way of testing whether what seems like good news in a given era is in fact the gospel.

— Leander Keck, *The Bible in the Pulpit*

---

to our everyday lives. But good preaching takes its point of view and its understanding of God and human beings and the world from the Scriptures — if not, it cannot be called "good."

Obviously, too, no preacher, no matter how fine, can command God to work through a sermon from the Bible. God acts when and where he desires.

The Spirit blows where he wills, Jesus said (John 3:8), and none of us can order him about. But the preacher who does not preach the Bible's viewpoint has abandoned the medium that God himself has chosen through which to work among us. The preacher has thereby cut off the congregation from a true knowledge and experience of God and of his work among them. Accordingly, your committee will want to examine each candidate carefully to determine whether or not he or she is forming his or her sermons from the Bible.

Strange Things Can Be Done to the Bible

Unfortunately, some clergy almost totally ignore the Bible's message when they preach, delivering instead what have been called "helpful hints for hurtful habits." Sermons of this kind usually have titles like "Five Ways to Control Your Anger" and "Making the Most of Your Time." Such sermons are based on modern mental-health principles or on the latest popular psychology, and they end up recommending a sort of "*Reader's Digest* religion" that has almost nothing to do with the Christian faith. Certainly mental health and psychology are important, but they

> *We have a fixed faith to preach, . . . and we are sent forth with a definite message fr. . . . God. We are not left to fabricate the message as we go along.*
>
> — C. H. Spurgeon, *Lectures to My Students*

are not the Word of God, and the pulpit has its own, more important message to proclaim.

Other clergy will entertain you with clever stories, or will try to manipulate your emotions with long, inspirational tales that bring tears to your eyes but that may or may not have anything to do with the Scripture reading for the day. Some clergy will preach their particular ideology or their brand of politics divorced from any basis in the Scripture reading. Those who ignore the Bible altogether may take as their text for the day a hymn or a poem or a quotation from some prominent person. Always a preacher's words have to be weighed against the Word of God in the Bible. Are the preacher's thoughts coming from the Scripture lesson and illumining and applying that Scripture, or are they simply the preacher's or society's opinions?

Then, too, some preachers may seem to be

preaching from the Bible when in fact they are only using a phrase or a verse from the Bible as a springboard to jump off into their own particular brand of piety. I once heard a sermon that took as its text Psalm 107:43: "Whoever is wise, let him give heed to these things, let men consider the steadfast love of the Lord." In context, "these things" is a reference to the works of God that have been recounted in the preceding forty-two verses of the psalm. But the sermon never mentioned those! Instead, it dwelt solely on what the *preacher* considered to be evidences of God's steadfast love.

Non-biblical preachers come in many varieties. There are those preachers who are allegorists. That is, they make something which is quite plain in the biblical text stand for something entirely different.

The Word of God! Give me back my Word, the Judge will say on the last day. When you think what certain people will have to unpack on that occasion, it's no laughing matter, I assure you!

— Georges Bernanos,
Diary of a Country Priest

For instance, when an allegorist uses Genesis 37:24, in which Joseph is cast by his brothers into the pit, he or she may make that pit stand for our spiritual condition: "All the world's in a pit." Other preachers psychologize the text. For example, they may expound at length on the psychological condition and inner thoughts of Judas after he betrayed Jesus, whereas the Bible says little about the subject, and the preacher's exposition is pure speculation. Or you will find sentimental clergy who preach only peace and loveliness and quiet, ignoring the Bible's realistic portrayals of the violence and ugliness and turmoil of actual human life. Then there are those preachers who, in their pride, elevate themselves above the Word of God, criticizing the Bible's point of view or correcting it and telling you what "actually happened."

As you listen to various preachers, ask yourself if they are placing themselves, along with the congregation, under the authority of the biblical text. Are the thoughts and viewpoint of Scripture determining the thoughts and viewpoint of the sermon, or is the preacher imposing his or her views on the Scripture lesson to make it say what it does not say, or to add to or subtract from its message? The Christian church must live from its Scriptures, or it will not live at all.

You Are Calling Your Resident Theologian

The theology of the Christian church is simply the statement, formulated in an orderly way, of what the Bible says to us about God the Father, Son, and Holy Spirit, about human beings, and about the world. And that theology has a specific content. As Christians, we confess a specific creed or belief. The earliest confession of the New Testament church, preserved for us by the apostle Paul, was "Jesus is Lord" (Rom. 10:9; 1 Cor. 12:3; Phil. 2:11). But as the church lived in the world it became necessary to define that statement more fully. So in the following centuries the church set forth its faith in the two confessions known as the Nicene Creed and the Apostles' Creed. Those two creeds summarize for us the basic content of the Christian Gospel as it is found in the Scriptures.

The person you are calling to be your minister is the one who should be trained in and committed to teaching you the meaning of those creeds for your daily life. Your minister will be your resident theologian, so to speak, the one who will clarify the content of the Christian faith for you, who will answer your questions about it, who will wrestle with you over the perplexities it raises for the way you live, and who will, Sunday after Sunday, proclaim to you the essential tenets of Christian belief.

*We have to deal with [those] who will be
either lost or saved, and they certainly will
not be saved by erroneous doctrine. . . .
What we have been taught of God we
teach. If we do not do this, we are not fit
for our position.*

— C. H. Spurgeon, *Lectures to My Students*

Therefore, as you read through dossiers and recommendations, as you conduct interviews and visit
churches to listen to candidates for your pulpit,
measure what you are reading and hearing against
the content of the Nicene and Apostles' creeds. What
does the candidate say about Jesus Christ? Does she
or he think Jesus was just a good man or an out-
standing prophet, or does the candidate believe Jesus
is Lord, "the only begotten Son of God"? Does he
or she think Jesus simply furnished us with an example of how to live and love, or does the candidate
believe that Jesus came down "for our salvation" and
"was crucified also for us"? Does the candidate you
are considering believe that Christ really "rose again
from the dead and ascended into heaven" and that
he will come again "to judge the quick and the

dead," or are the resurrection and the second coming non-essentials in the faith of your candidate? What

---

The "work of an evangelist" does not consist in proclaiming "ideals." It does not consist in criticizing man, his failures, his weaknesses, or his arrogance. . . . It consists in proclaiming the Evangel. The proclamation of the gospel is the proclamation of Jesus Christ.

— Karl Barth, *God in Action*

---

your candidate believes about Christ will largely determine everything else she or he believes and preaches.

Who is God for your candidate? Is he "the Father Almighty, Maker of heaven and earth" and Lord over nature and history, as the Bible has it, or is God some benign spirit contained in all things and persons? How does God make himself known to human beings? Is this a revelation that comes primarily through the story of Jesus Christ? Or can the God of your candidate be known immediately from the natural world, making the biblical story unnecessary?

How does your candidate understand the role of the Holy Spirit? Does he or she consider the Spirit so important that he or she rarely mentions the Father and the Son? Or does the candidate clearly believe that the Holy Spirit "proceeds from the Father and the Son"?

How does the person you are considering understand the nature of the church and of the "communion of saints"? What does the candidate think Christians have to do in the world? Does your candidate preach moralistic sermons that are peppered with "should" and "ought" and "must," and that largely urge listeners to get out there and "do good," and so save themselves? Or does the candidate believe that God's help is necessary in order to lead the Christian life?

All of these questions deal with the heart of Christian belief, and you will want to ask them of each candidate you are considering before you issue the call to your pulpit. Listen carefully to the answers given, even if you yourself could not formulate replies. Can the candidate answer theological questions in a clear and simple manner, or does the candidate seem to be uncertain about what he or she believes? I once knew a minister who, when asked a theological question related to everyday life, could only giggle and change the subject in reply. Certainly such

> *The purpose of theology is to glorify God, to save human souls, to transform human life and society.*
>
> —John Leith, *John Calvin's Doctrine of the Christian Life*

a person is not going to be able to answer your questions about your faith. The clearer Christian theology is in the candidate's mind, the better he or she can teach it to you. "I am not ashamed," wrote Paul, "for I know whom I have believed" (2 Tim. 1:12). Seek a "resident theologian" for your church who has that same sure belief.

A related point: you will want to question each candidate for your pulpit about his or her personal study habits. Is the candidate continuing to grow in knowledge and understanding of the Christian faith? Has he or she read a book dealing with theology in the last three months? What was the book, and what did the candidate learn from it? Who is the candidate's favorite theologian, and what is that theologian's main position? The study habits of some candidates may be very narrow in scope. For example, Reinhold Niebuhr once wrote that "the ministry is the only profession in which you can make a virtue of ignorance. If you have read nothing but commentaries for twenty years, that is supposed to invest you with an aura of sanctity and piety" (see *Leaves from the Notebook of a Tamed Cynic*). And indeed, biblical

---

A manse without a study would be comparable to a church without a pulpit, and the efficiency of the pulpit is commensurate with the efficiency of the study.

— David Smith, *The Art of Preaching*

---

commentaries — plus, perhaps, a few popular novels — are all that some preachers have read since they left seminary!

Does your candidate also read widely in good literature? There is nothing that develops a preacher's imagination, creativity, and style of speech so much as delving into fine prose and poetry. Nor is there any practice that more enlarges a minister's sympathy for and understanding of the human race than the regular reading of fine literary works. Does a particular candidate explore the wisdom of the human race that is contained in good books? If so, you may have a jewel on your hands.

Finally, try to get some sense of each candidate's long-term commitment to learning. One of the provisions that should be written into every preacher's call is two weeks of study leave per year. Ask each candidate how she or he would use that two weeks of time free from the congregation. The answer to the question may tell you a great deal about a candidate's desire to continue learning.

Is the Knowledge Real or Rote?

You will also want to know how deeply a candidate's learning has affected his or her personal life. The prophet Isaiah once pronounced God's judgment on Israel

> because this people draw near with their mouth
>   and honor me with their lips,
> while their hearts are far from me,
> and their fear of me is a commandment of men
>   learned by rote.
>
> (29:13)

Obviously, it is quite possible to say all of the theologically correct words about the Christian faith and never have those words affect one's heart or life. Indeed, the Bible tells us that the devil is very adept at quoting Scripture (Matt. 4:1-11).

This does not mean, of course, that a candidate should not know the Scriptures. The more a person is saturated with the knowledge of the Word of God, the more likely that person is to live and move and have his or her being in that Word. So question each candidate closely about his or her knowledge. Is the person gradually enlarging her or his understanding of the Scriptures by continual and systematic study of them? What is the candidate's favorite psalm and why? What can the candidate tell you about God's covenants in the Bible? What does he or she know about Isaiah of Jerusalem (Isaiah 1–39) or about the Suffering Servant in Isaiah 40–55? How would the candidate characterize the book of Romans or Hebrews or Revelation? What is his or her favorite passage in the letters of Paul? If asked to tell children a story of Jesus, which story would he or she choose?

But when you are examining a candidate's knowledge of theology and of the Scriptures, you want to find out how much that knowledge has mattered in his or her own life. In short, what is the personal piety of the individual? Is his or her personal life shaped by Scripture and Christian theology, or are those just "commandments of men learned by rote"? Does the person have a discipline of regular prayer? If so, have him or her describe it. Can the person tell you of some personal incident when the Scriptures made a difference in his or her life? How does he or she regard the commandments of Jesus and of Paul? What would be his or her description of a Christian life? Does the candidate feel he or she is growing in Christian maturity, or does he or she already have all the answers or feel that he or she has essentially "mastered" the Christian lifestyle?

There is nothing more difficult than trying to judge the nature of someone's personal piety. I was once a member of a PNC that came face to face with

---

One who preaches God's Word and is not himself comforted, strengthened, rebuked, and humbled by it is like a man who sits by a spring and goes thirsty, who has bread in his hands and goes hungry.

— Karl Buechsel, *Erinnerungen aus den Leben eines Landgeistlichen*

---

this difficulty. We thought we had found a committed and practicing Christian who could preach

> *A minister of Christ should have his tongue, his heart, and his hand agree.*
>
> — Jerome, *Ad Nepotianum*

wonderful sermons, but after several years in our pulpit, he deserted his wife and four children and ran off with the female superintendent of the Sunday school! It is very hard to know what is in the human heart. We might have had a hint, however, if we had inquired about the man's actions in his previous parish, and that is something you will want to do.

You committee members know something of the practice of the Christian life in your own daily round. On the basis of your experience in living by the Word of God, try to probe a candidate's heart and mind to discover if the commitment to Christ's way is genuine or superficial.

Try to Forget the Stereotypes

One of the difficulties that the Jews had with Jesus was that he did not act as they thought the Messiah should act; consequently, they crucified him for blasphemy. Unfortunately, we, like those Jews, often carry around with us stereotypes of what the truly religious life should look like. Some of us, for example, think that a religious person should always glow with some inner light or always be calm and serene, but there are a lot of fine Christians who would not meet those requirements. Others think that a truly religious person will never break certain man-made rules: I knew one parish that objected to the pastor's young wife wearing shorts in summer! Such superficiality was roundly condemned by our Lord. "You leave the commandment of God," he charged, "and hold fast the tradition of men" (Mark 7:8).

The important thing is to try to assess a candidate's character by fundamental criteria, and probably among the best guides for that are the Ten Commandments found in Exodus 20:1-17. That Decalogue, found also in Deuteronomy 5:6-21 and confirmed by our Lord (Mark 10:17-21 and parallels), made up the basic commandments of Israel's life, commandments apart from which Israel could not be the covenant people of God.

Committed Christians try to follow God's commandments, not in order to win God's favor but because God has already redeemed them and made them his own in Jesus Christ (cf. Exod. 20:2). Out of gratitude and thanksgiving for redemption, a Christian person will not commit adultery, or steal (does the candidate pay bills on time?), or bear false witness by any word of mouth, or covet anything that is a neighbor's. A true Christian will honor his or her parents, and will seek a day of rest from labor for all persons one day a week, and will not substitute the worship of something or someone else for the worship of the one true God. In short, a Christian person will have God at the center of his or her life, and will seek to subordinate everything else to that loyalty.

Like a "two-edged sword" that pierces to "soul and spirit" (Heb. 4:12), those commandments help us judge the Christian character of a candidate. For

---

The ambitious preacher is a pestilence to the church.

— Martin Luther, *Tischreden*

---

example, they help us judge ambition. Is a candidate's main goal to climb up the ladder of so-called success by gradually moving from smaller churches into the prestigious pulpit of a large congregation? That is covetousness. Or does a candidate preach himself rather than preaching Jesus Christ as Lord and himself as your servant for Jesus' sake (2 Cor. 4:5)? That is a violation of the first of the Ten Commandments. Will a candidate take a stand on the Word of God

---

An office-bearer who wants something other than to obey his King is unfit to bear his office.

— Abraham Kuyper,
Die Kirche Jesu Christi

---

when opposition arises, or will he or she give in to pressure for the sake of furthering his or her career? Where is a candidate's heart when career and money and status are at stake?

So too, the Decalogue helps us assess family life. Is a candidate's family life marked by honor, respect of personhood, and discipline of character? Surely no congregation will call an adulterer or one who violates marriage vows in word or deed. But you also need to ask what is at the center of a candidate's family. Is it the love and knowledge of God in Jesus Christ, taught to children and practiced by parents? Do a candidate's family members also seem to know what it means to live the Christian life in the fellowship of the church? One of my professors in Europe once remarked that too many clergy were marrying "obstacles" to the Gospel. And 1 Timothy 3:5 adds to that: "If a man [or woman] does not know how to manage his [or her] own household, how can he [or she] care for God's church?" It is a good question to keep in mind. "You will know them by their fruits," Jesus said (Matt. 7:16).

In line with that, vow to write into the terms of call to your new minister one day of rest a week — barring a death or serious emergency in the congregation — when the minister will be totally free to spend time with his or her family. Some church members seem to resent it when their minister is off on a family outing rather than at their beck and call, but ministers' families too need time together in order to be whole and Christian. Ministers' responsibilities to their families, like yours, are an integral part of their service to God and his church.

The Single and the Divorced

Seminary placement services have a very hard time finding calls for unmarried individuals. It still seems to be a twisted assumption in our society, despite our multiplicity of single households, that there's something wrong with single people. But there is a large place for single persons in the Gospel — neither Jesus nor Paul was married — and it may be that a single person has been called by God to that role. Or it may be that God has not yet led him or her to the person he or she is destined to marry.

Then too, it is still the assumption in some churches that when they call a person to their pulpit, they are gaining, without pay, the time and talents of the spouse as well — an assumption that may make them less inclined to call the single candidate. Stereotypes, especially of minister's wives and the role they are to play in the congregation, die hard. Some congregations just assume that of course the minister's wife will teach Sunday school or lead the women's group or organize the Wednesday-night suppers. But God may have a very different role in mind for that spouse. And PNCs must not let past customs and unjust stereotypes shut out the possibility that God may be calling a single person to their pulpit.

More difficult is the issue of dealing with divorced clergy. Unfortunately, in our time many seminary graduates and many clergy already in the field have been divorced. That should not be an *automatic* reason for disqualifying a candidate. There are some legiti-

> *Evangelism is witness. It is one beggar telling another where to get food. The Christian does not offer out of his bounty. He has no bounty. He is simply guest at his Master's table and, as evangelist, he calls others too.*
>
> — Daniel T. Niles

mate reasons for divorce from a spouse, such as chronic alcoholism, abuse, persistent infidelity, and mental illness; I know divorced clergy who have suffered one or another of all of these tragedies. But your committee will want to investigate frankly and thoroughly a candidate's reasons for divorcing, because those reasons can be a good indication of character. You want a minister who can perform a marriage ceremony with integrity, who knows how to deal in a Christian manner with the conflicts that arise in every marriage, and who is always willing to bear his or her share of suffering for the sake of the Gospel. Divorced persons may or may not have those qualifications, but you need to question them closely to find out. Once again, the importance of keeping your findings confidential cannot be stressed too strongly.

As You Listen to Sermons

You have weeded out some of the candidates for your pulpit on the basis of dossiers, telephone interviews, and recommendations from others. You may continue the process of elimination by listening to tapes of sermons that the candidates have sent you. Certainly such tapes can help you determine whether or not a candidate is preaching sermons of biblical and theological substance — the kind of sermons that will feed your congregation weekly with the Word of God. But after you have narrowed down your list of candidates, there is no substitute for visiting a candidate's church unannounced to worship and to see and to hear him or her in the pulpit. (You will want to make sure that the candidate is preaching on the Sunday of your visit.)

Everyone hears a sermon differently. A particular sermon will speak meaningfully to one person but will leave another unaffected — God works in mysterious ways. It is therefore wise for at least two and preferably three of you to visit a church together and then to compare notes afterward.

Keep in mind, however, that no preacher delivers a really fine sermon every Sunday of the year. The best preacher may have had to preside over three funerals during the week and be unprepared on the

Sunday you visit. Sometimes, too, the Spirit simply does not choose to work, and the selected biblical text has not yielded its best fruit. Therefore, if a candidate you are seriously interested in delivers a less than stellar sermon, visit his or her church again or have other members of the committee do so. Or listen again to the tape the preacher sent you and compare it to what you heard when you visited. If the taped sermon seems much better than what you heard "live," by all means visit the candidate's church again.

Remain as inconspicuous as possible in a congregation. Behave like any other visitors, and avoid mentioning to the members there that you are on a PNC. But do try to engage some of the members in conversation, perhaps during the coffee hour before or after the service. Listen to what the members say about their preacher. And be sensitive to the atmosphere of feeling in the congregation. Do the members seem indifferent or enthusiastic about their church? Does the congregation seem to be alive or dead?

Beyond the subjective impressions that you pick up by attending a church, however, there are more objective assessments you can make by using basic criteria for preaching that separate good sermons from bad. You will want to take notice of the following:

Most important, as I have previously emphasized, is this question: Does the sermon depend on the viewpoint of the Scripture lesson that has been read? But — also important — does the preacher relate the biblical point of view to your life and the life of the congregation in a meaningful way? One man said of his preacher, "I get so tired of being talked to as if I

Think of the news [preachers] are ordained to declare. That God has invaded history with power and great glory; that in the day of man's terrible need a second Adam has come forth to the fight and to the rescue; that in the cross the supreme triumph of naked evil has been turned once for all to irrevocable defeat; that Christ is alive now and present through his Spirit; that through the risen Christ there has been let loose into the world a force which can transform life beyond recognition — that is the most momentous message human lips were ever charged to speak.

— James Stewart, Heralds of God

---

were a Corinthian." His preacher was talking about the Bible, but his message all concerned the past. Does the sermon present the God of the Bible as active here and now in your life? Does the preacher use illustrations and language which make that activity clear? Does the speech the preacher uses enable you to picture in your mind's eye who God in Christ is and what he is doing, has done, and will do?

Does the sermon deal mostly with God, or is it all about human beings? Many preachers spend most of their sermon time dwelling on human problems and never get around to saying what God is doing about them. It is easy to present the problems — all of us can read the morning headlines and tell what is wrong in our world. But it takes a preacher to tell what God is doing about the wrongs, and that activity of God should be the primary content of the sermon.

When dealing with human wrong, does the sermon exaggerate the sin of the people in the pews so that they end up sounding as if they were the worst of reprobates? Or, conversely, does the sermon assume that the congregation is without sin? In short, are human beings pictured realistically? Does the preacher seem to know human life as it actually is? Does he or she use illustrations that have to do with common people? Does the preacher seem to be aware of the actual nature of the world in which we live?

Is the sermon logically structured so that you can trace its argument? It is a good practice to outline what you hear so that later you can review the sermon's content and also report back to the full

---

Unless the man [or woman] in the pulpit has felt the deep hurt and heartache of humanity — its bitter, blinding tragedy — unless he [or she] knows the rough places, the dangerous turns, the dismal stretches of the old, winding road, and something of what the pilgrims carry in their packs, he [or she] cannot minister to our need, much less lead us far along the way whither we seek to go.

— Joseph Fort Newton, *The New Preaching*

---

committee. Outlining will help you decide if you have heard solid material or fluff. There are some preachers who *sound* marvelous, but when you outline what they actually said, you realize how little of real value they communicated. You discover that they are silver-tongued orators who have said nothing essential to the Gospel.

Many a man in his aspirations to be literary has rather qualified himself to write reviews rather than to preach sermons. A quaint evangelist was wont to say that Christ hung crucified beneath Greek, Latin, and Hebrew.

— C. H. Spurgeon, *Lectures to My Students*

Does the sermon keep your interest until its end? Does it move along steadily, or does the preacher get bogged down telling a long story or quoting a long hymn or poem so that you lose the train of thought? Is it only some striking illustration that remains in your mind at the end of the sermon? If so, does that illustration convey the meaning of the Scripture reading for the day?

Does the sermon appeal to your heart as well as to your mind, or does it seem more like a lecture to you? On the other hand, does the sermon provide food for thought as well as inspiration? Does the sermon help you see in your mind's eye what the Christian life looks like?

Pulpit Stance and Delivery

Much of the effectiveness of good preaching has to do not only with sermon content but also with the person speaking the words and the manner in which they are spoken. As Richard Baxter, a nineteenth-century clergyman, once wrote, "So great a God, whose message we deliver, should be honored by our delivery of it." Accordingly, you may want to pay close attention to technique.

Does the preacher seem comfortable in the pulpit? If you are listening to someone who has only recently graduated from seminary, you may find that he or she seems somewhat nervous, but you should not be too quick to chalk that up as a demerit — most young graduates quickly overcome their nervousness as they gain experience. But if the

---

A corroding and deadening sin is professionalism, which shows itself in an affected tone of voice, a studied manner, a use of conventional phrases, and an unholy familiarity with spiritual things.

— John Watson, The Cure of Souls

---

preacher has been in the pulpit for a number of years and still seems as tense as a cat watching an approaching dog, then he or she has problems. On the other hand, you do not want a preacher who slouches around the chancel, drapes himself or herself over the pulpit, and appears lackadaisical and indifferent. Nor do you want one who speaks in a whispered, pious tone and moves with such lethargy that you think he or she is going to expire at any moment. Good preachers bring energy to their sermons; their adrenaline is flowing because preaching is a very exciting calling!

It is very important to notice if the preacher seems to be speaking *to* the congregation. Is he or

---

Nonsense does not improve by being bellowed.

— C. H. Spurgeon, *Lectures to My Students*

---

she actually addressing the gathered people, responding to their silent reactions, reaching each one of them with words that are loud and clear enough to be heard even by the elderly? Does the preacher look directly at the congregation and make eye contact with them? Or are the preacher's eyes glued to a manuscript or to a space above the congregation's heads or to one wall or window of the sanctuary?

Along the same lines, does the preacher speak in a basically conversational tone (raised, of course, in volume), or does he or she have a preaching singsong or monotone or even a shout that bears little resemblance to ordinary speech between people?

What attitude does the preacher seem to have toward the congregation? Is it belligerent, as if the

---

To confront other people without being confronted oneself leads to insufferable pretensions of righteousness.

— Reinhold Niebuhr, *Justice and Mercy*

---

members of the congregation were adversaries or the preacher had a chip on her or his shoulder? Or does the preacher seem to love and respect and care about her or his people, speaking to them, even in judgment, in the tones of a true shepherd? Does the preacher identify with the people, speaking in terms of "we" and "us" and "you and I," or do you get the impression that the minister thinks he or she and God are on one side and the congregation is on the other? Does the preacher inspire in you a feeling of trust, so that you might want to go to him or her when you have a problem or question? Would you want this preacher as a model for your child? Would you want him or her to be present during the most intimate events of your life — at a baptism, a marriage ceremony, or a funeral service?

Finally, does the preacher have a voice and gestures that you think you and your congregation could live with, Sunday after Sunday? I put it in those terms because, while voice and body language are important in the pulpit, they are not all-important. One of the greatest preachers of the past generation stuttered and plucked frequently at the sleeve of his robe. Another had a high little voice but spoke marvelous words from God. Some preachers flail about with their hands because they are so wrapped up in what they are saying; others remain almost motionless in their pulpits. Probably the best question to ask with regard to voice and gestures is this: Does the preacher appear to be herself or himself in the pulpit? Are you listening to and seeing a genuine human being, or does the preacher seem to be putting on a dramatic act for the congregation's benefit? Preaching is not a performance. It is one person speaking in truth and with sincerity and conviction to other people about the deep things of God.

The Context of Worship

Preaching in the Christian church is an integral part of worship, offered to God as part of our service to him. As Luther once said, "I have never been troubled because I cannot preach well, but I have often been afraid and awed to think that I have to preach before God's face of his great majesty and divine being." Preaching is part of our worship before the throne of our glorious King. Accordingly, when you listen to a candidate preach in a church service, you will want to note how he or she relates the sermon to the entire worship of that divine Sovereign.

Does the whole service hang together, perhaps

The moment some [enter] the pulpit . . . they leave their own personal [selfhood] behind them, and become . . . official. . . . There they might almost boast with the Pharisee that they are not as other men are, although it would be blasphemy to thank God for it.

— C. H. Spurgeon, *Lectures to My Students*

shaped by one principal theme, or does it seem to be a disjointed collection of acts and words unrelated to one another? Does the service show careful planning around the Scripture reading for the day so that not only the sermon but also the prayers, music, and other portions of the liturgy seem to arise out of that reading and be connected with it?

On the other hand, does the service provide opportunity for the full range of Christian worship? Is there a place for the confession of sin as well as for praise? Is there opportunity for silent prayer on the congregation's part as well as for the minister's prayers? Would the service minister to one who mourns as well as to one who rejoices? Does the service include the whole company of the congregation, or would the elderly and children, or the poor and suffering, feel somehow left out of the liturgy?

Is the sermon made the climax of the service so that nothing else important seems to happen until the preacher gets up to speak? Or is there a sense during the worship service that the whole congregation stands before Almighty God, rendering to him its sacrifices of praise and thanksgiving in glorification of his holy presence?

How does the sermon accord with the sacraments of the church? Whether or not a baptism is performed or the Lord's Supper is observed on the

> *It ought not to be possible to conduct a church service in a way which leaves a stranger with the impression that nothing particular is happening and that no important business is on hand.*
>
> — James Stewart, *Heralds of God*

Sunday that you attend a candidate's worship service, ask yourself if what you see and hear accords with and reinforces the sacraments. Could the content of the sermon be confirmed by the sacrament of the Supper? Or does the sermon seem to contradict everything that would be celebrated in the Lord's Supper — its sacrifice for sin, its gift of new life, its communion of the people with one another and with their Lord, its expectation of Christ's coming again? Similarly, does the sermon confirm you in your baptism as a member of Christ's body, freed from the bondage of sin and death and pledged to lead the new life of the redeemed? Or does the sermon leave you indifferent about affirming and living out your baptism in your daily life as one who belongs to God?

You will also want to notice very carefully how

a candidate conducts the worship service. Does she or he read Scripture in such a manner that its meaning and primary emphases are made clear to you? Has the candidate apparently practiced the Scripture reading ahead of time, or does he or she stumble over words or mispronounce them? If the latter is true, that particular minister is not taking Scripture very seriously.

Also ask yourself if the preacher is worshiping *with* the congregation. Is he or she constantly fiddling with papers, estimating the attendance, smiling at someone in the pews, or being otherwise distracted? Or do you gain the sense that the preacher knows that all of you are standing before a glorious God? Unless the preacher as worship leader has that sense and communicates it to you, he or she cannot lead you in worship.

Finally, does the preacher utter prayers to the God who is present with you, or are the prayers largely directed to the congregation instead, so that sometimes God is even referred to in the prayers in the third person? Do the prayers tell God what to do, as if he were not the Lord of our lives and of all nature and history, or are the prayers sincere offerings of heartfelt praise and confession, petition and gratitude? Do the prayers, like the sermon, arise out of biblical understandings of who God is? Do they give

> *In the ministry of the gospel, prayer is*
> *no less powerful than preaching. He,*
> *therefore, who cannot pray, cannot be*
> *a perfect minister. For the things of God*
> *should be laid before men, but men's*
> *affairs before God.*
>
> —Johann Albrecht Bengel,
> *Gnomon Novi Testamenti*

you the impression that the preacher knows the God to whom he or she is praying? No one can preach or practice the Christian life or lead anyone else in the faith unless that person also knows how to pray and does it faithfully every day.

Do Not Be Too Hasty or Easily Satisfied

Sometimes great pressure is put on a pulpit nominating committee to get its job done so that the congregation is not left without a minister for too long. Sometimes a PNC is even pressured not to spend too much money. In such circumstances the temptation is to forget some of the criteria we have discussed and to settle for a preacher who seems at least adequate. While you do not want the nominating process to stretch out endlessly, you also should not surrender to the notion

---

Remember, O Lord, what thou hast wrought in us, and not what we deserve; and as thou hast called us to thy service, make us worthy of our calling.

— Leonine Sacramentary

---

that no one can live up to all of these criteria of good preaching. Yes, many candidates can. There are hundreds of fine ministers out there in the church who are truly preaching the Gospel of Jesus Christ. There are many young graduates just leaving seminary who are well-qualified to fill your pulpit. Therefore, persevere in your search. Pray over it. Check out possible candidates whom individuals outside of your committee may recommend to you. Consult with seminary professors and church leaders whom you trust to get candidates' names. Read dossiers thoroughly and listen carefully to the sermon tapes sent to you. Always ask God for guidance.

If you can recommend a good preacher to fill your pulpit, you will bring blessing on your lives and the lives of your fellow church members for years. You will influence the course of the Christian church. Above all, you will further the spread of the Good News of Jesus Christ. "Faith comes from what is heard," says Paul (Rom. 10:17), "and what is heard comes by the preaching of Christ." But how is anyone to hear without a preacher?

Now to him who by the power at work within us is able to do far more abundantly than all that we ask or think, to him be glory in the church and in Christ Jesus to all generations, for ever and ever. Amen.